AMELIA SAINT GEORGE'S
Patchwork, Quilting & Appliqué

AMELIA SAINT GEORGE'S
Patchwork, Quilting & Appliqué

HarperCollins*Publishers*

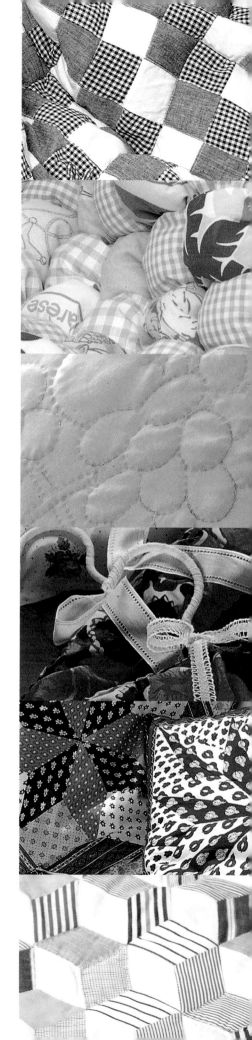

*To my cats, eleven year old Prince Andrew and
six year old Lady Gray, for all the welcoming greetings
and long quiet hours spent together.*

First published in 1997
by HarperCollins*Publishers*, London

97 99 01 03 02 00 98
1 3 5 7 9 8 6 4 2

A catalogue record for this book is
available from the British Library

Editor: Heather Dewhurst
Designer: Rachel Smyth
Photographer: John Freeman

ISBN 0 00 413300 5

Set in Goudy
Colour origination in Singapore, by Colourscan
Printed and bound in Italy by Rotolito Lombarda SpA, Milan

CONTENTS

INTRODUCTION

Patchwork, quilting and appliqué are crafts that can be used on their own to create individual projects, or interlinked with each other to produce one magnificent project. In this book, I have introduced these three techniques with the help of several quick and easy projects and showed how they can be used together in imaginative ways to create a range of decorative and innovative items, ranging from traditional cushions and quilts to tablecloths and towels. With the templates provided within some projects and on tracing paper at the back of the book, and full explanations for each project, you will soon be able to start stitching.

Getting started

Begin by playing with little scraps of fabric that are just too big to throw away; striped shirts with worn collars and dashing summer shorts with frayed edges can quickly become perfect materials for patchwork, quilting and appliqué. Most of these projects re-use old clothing. Sumptuous old silk ties, outgrown skirts and corners of linen sheets and tablecloths are recycled and transformed into unique creations. It is easy to experiment when the materials and equipment are inexpensive; there is little to lose but much to gain.

All the projects give clear instructions, together with tips for how to cut corners and still achieve the very best results. Some of the projects are quick and simple to do; others, although not requiring much more skill, are more time-consuming, particularly if you complete them by hand, and they will challenge the most experienced stitchers.

Choosing a project

I do my patchwork while travelling in the car, on a train or on a plane, when sitting in the park while the children play, in front of the television, or listening to the radio. Like so many people I meet, I like to have something in my hands all the time, and I am much calmer while sewing intriguing coloured fabrics together, remembering old clothes that are now in smaller pieces for me to transform into another patchwork, quilt or appliqué.

While playing with so many different ideas for this book, it was hard to limit the selection to 20 or so projects which demonstrated all the essential sewing techniques and used a wide variety of fabrics from silk and cotton, to felt and fleece. However, I did choose a selection, and the result is a wide diversity of projects with something for everyone. So, whether you want to make a charming baby's puff quilt that is light, warm and durable, a tea-time tablecloth of striped *trompe-l'oeil* cubes, or a set of imaginative beach towels in bright appliquéd colours, there is a project in this book for you!

This stylish yet simple block quilt is made with patches of men's shirts and enlivened with amusing appliqué animals.

Foundations and inspirations

Compatability of fabrics, weights and textures is an individual challenge frequently influenced by current decorative taste and fashion. Many new materials have been developed in the last 20 years and gone are the days that children are sent off to school in itchy tweeds. Now there is a huge variety of fabric easily available, ranging from vibrant non-itchy tweeds to delicate man-made fabrics. When planning any project within the book, use my choice of fabrics only as a guide, as I often choose those fabrics that are nearest to hand.

All the techniques within this book were traditionally born out of necessity: patchwork grew from making more material out of precious scraps; quilting developed from the need to create warm clothing; while appliqué was a result of patching holes. So do not be inhibited if you are told that your patchwork design is not traditional since it has not been made from floral fabric, or that only 20 designs are 'correct' for quilting, or that appliqué should always be completed by hand. All these wonderfully expressive and ancient sewing crafts are waiting for you to play with, so spread out your mixed bunch of materials and enjoy yourself cutting, snipping, pinning and sewing, either by machine or by hand.

Choosing fabrics

Colour and textile combinations in patchwork, quilting and appliqué must be thought through carefully before you begin. If you are using recycled men's shirts, sort them into different types, for example, thicker shirts for country or contemporary wear, or finer city striped shirts,

the sort I chose for the patchwork tablecloth (see page 54). Keeping to the same texture throughout a quilt will give it a very elegant finish. Alternatively, combining textures within a quilt will produce a playful feel, as in the animal quilt (see page 80), in which I combined fine city shirts and textured country shirts.

Recycling old clothes

When using recycled clothing, make sure that all the fabric has been pre-washed. Never be tempted to use material from an unreliable source without first washing it. Shrinking or bleeding dye fabric will ruin your work.

A new discovery for me when compiling this book was polyester felt. This fabric is washable and perfect for combining with many different textures of material. I used it to make the animals in the animal quilt (see page 80), the appliquéd seaweed on the towels (see page 90) and the fishes, boats and shells on the appliquéd cushions (see page 22).

With many differing textures able to combine well, it is difficult to give a list of dos and don'ts. However, when beginning, do restrict your texture combinations to three or four. Remember that stitching is a textile combination. If you limit your choice of colour too, this will produce greater harmony in your work and will result in a stitched heirloom that will give pleasure for years to come.

Patchwork, quilting and appliqué are relaxing occupations and can easily be completed while sitting out in the sunshine.

BASIC
TECHNIQUES

This section sets out all the basic techniques of patchwork, quilting and appliqué, enabling you to cut, piece and stitch the projects that follow.

Patchwork

Patchwork is both a versatile and creative craft. Born out of necessity with pieces of precious material being joined together for further use, patchwork soon developed into an art form. If you already make clothes you will no doubt have accumulated many offcuts of fabric that you can use for patchwork. Alternatively, you can easily make a collection of similar textures and weights of cloth, such as worn cotton shirts or silk ties, that can be used together in patchwork.

I was fascinated that some patchworks had a three-dimensional aspect, but found the explanations in various books difficult to follow and I did not achieve very rewarding results. So I have made a series of patterns (see Templates, page 96) which I feel confident you will have no difficulty using. Three-dimensional patchworks are not more difficult to make, but you do have to be more careful at the cutting-out stage. Some of the pattern pieces are the same shape and use the same fabric, but they have to be placed on the fabric in a different way so that the pattern of the fabric goes in a different direction.

Find some fabric that you really like for this project. Six different patterns of fabric are needed in two lots of dark, medium and light: one set for the cube and another for the background. The differences do not have to be as dramatic as mine but select something which suits your interior.

This patchwork cushion has a wonderful trompe-l'oeil *effect that is easily achieved using the pattern on page 97.*

Making a patchwork cushion

If you have never made a patchwork before, follow the instructions carefully and you should have no probems. One common fault to watch out for is not cutting your templates accurately; if you start off with a wobbly-edged template the fabric patches will not fit together properly and the result will be a mess! Another point worth noting is that for *trompe-l'oeil* patchwork it is important that you spend time aligning the templates on the fabric, making each patch identical. If you don't do this, then you will not achieve the right effect. Fold the fabric neatly on to the template and baste it down without distorting or pulling the fabric out of shape.

Everyone says that patchwork is easy for me because I know how to do it. What they do not know is that I have seven nieces and I test my ideas on them, and they frequently have a go. They were very zealous about pulling their stitching tight, which is not necessary, and most of them placed their pattern pieces incorrectly on to the base layout as I had done. However, like me, they corrected themselves. So don't be put off before you begin – we all had to make that first attempt! Once you begin, you will discover how easy it is.

MATERIALS

Six patterned cotton fabrics, each measuring 90cm x 30cm (36in x 12in)

Basting thread

Matching sewing thread

Backing fabric, 45cm x 45cm (18in x 18in)

Cushion backing, 45cm x 45cm (18in x 18in)

Cushion pad to fit

STEP ONE

Remove the template from page 97, enlarge it by 111 per cent, then photocopy it five times: four for each corner of the cushion and a fifth for use as a template. Cut out four of the photocopies accurately, to separate the individual patches.

STEP TWO

If you prefer to create templates out of scrap paper, copy the template from the book (enlarged by 111 per cent) on to postcard master templates. Mark each one accurately with both colour tone and, most importantly, with directional arrows.

STEP THREE

Lay out the templates on to the reverse side of the different fabrics in the direction of the nap or pattern. Line up the templates on the fabric so that each patch will be identical. Pin in place. Cut out the patches, leaving a small allowance for turning around the edges. For cotton fabric, allow 6mm (¼in); a thicker material may need more.

STEP FOUR

Turn over the small turning on to the paper templates and baste the turning down. Be careful not to stitch too firmly or you may distort the template.

STEP FIVE

Lay out the basted patches on to the fifth template to create a corner of the cushion. I decided that the white pattern with the navy design was facing in the wrong direction. Also the two pieces with the striped design did not match. Look carefully at the next step where both are corrected.

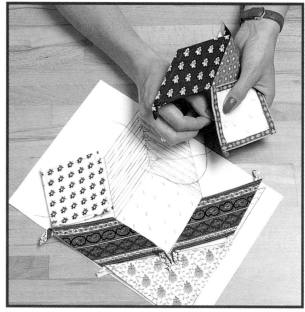

STEP SIX

Taking two adjoining patches at a time, place them right sides facing and stitch them together with a light but firm oversewing stitch, called whipping stitch. Continue to join all the patches together to form the quarter cushion. Then join all four quarters together to complete the patchwork cushion.

STEP SEVEN

It is traditional to finish off a patchwork by adding a border. This makes the patchwork larger and adds strength by having a solid piece of material around each side. To calculate the amount of fabric you need for the border, measure the length of the patchwork and multiply this by 4. Then measure the width of the border and multiply this by 8 for the mitred corners. Place the border piece and the patchwork together, right sides facing and edges matching, and stitch together using whipping stitch as before.

STEP EIGHT

Mitre each corner of the border in turn. To do this, leave one border piece flat and fold the other back diagonally at a 45° angle. Then pin to secure and slipstitch in place, checking that the pattern on the fabric lines up.

STEP NINE

Turn the patchwork over and carefully remove all the basting stitches and the paper templates. Now the full glory of your work will be revealed. To make the patchwork up into a cushion, first back the patchwork with matching fabric (to hide all the seams), then stitch this to a cushion backing, right sides facing, leaving a small gap. Turn the cover the right way out, insert a cushion pad, then slipstitch the gap closed. Alternatively, you can make a flap-over cushion (see page 62).

Machine-quilting

Quilting was originally developed as a way of guaranteeing warmth. When homes were not heated, items of clothing were frequently quilted including, at one time, women's underskirts and bodices. Coats did not exist as we know them today as the difference between interior and exterior warmth was not so dramatic and the trick was to stay warm all the time. Small children were often sewn into waddings under bodies like a thick vest, which in poorer households were only cut off in the spring.

Nowadays, machine-quilting has more or less taken over from traditional hand-quilting and has become a decorative art in its own right. It is quick and easy to do, even with a simple sewing machine. Excellent results can be achieved by feeding the rolled sandwich of fabric under a looser machine tension, and you can finish a quilt in an afternoon.

You can quilt on many different types of fabric, but plain-coloured fabrics will always show up the quilting more than patterned fabrics. But, whether quilting flowered patterns within the fabric or tracing designs on to a plain fabric, the results look delightfully decorative and still trap the heat. The fabric I chose to quilt is actually printed as a patchwork; checked fabrics are also excellent to use as the lines are easy to follow. For an example of quilting decorative designs on plain fabric, see the cushions on page 38.

A blue and white quilt hangs out to air in the morning breeze, and two compass cushions nestle in the cockpit. The crisp designs are practical, durable and fun on board.

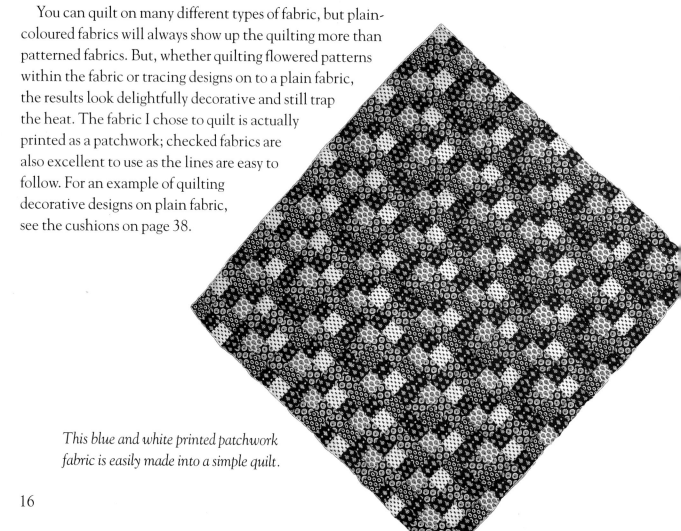

This blue and white printed patchwork fabric is easily made into a simple quilt.

Making a quilt

Quilting is quick and easy to achieve using a sewing machine. A simple machine quilt like this one can be completed in an afternoon and is very inexpensive to make. The sewing machine I use is a very basic model but more advanced machines may have extra quilting gadgets which simplify the process, so consult your handbook before starting the project.

One of the easiest ways to quilt is on pre-printed fabric squares like these, where you can simply stitch straight lines along the sides of the squares, rather than following a curving pattern. Once you have become accustomed to this simple quilting, you can progress on to more adventurous quilting patterns. I have noticed many differing fabrics appearing on the market which are ideal for quilting, even speciality Christmas designs, so hunt around for exceptional effects.

Alternatively, you can make your own patchwork quilt following one of the projects in this book, and machine-quilt this in the same way. In addition to adding textural decoration to the fabric, quilting makes the fabric warm and cosy and exceptionally durable, with each layer of fabric supporting the next.

MATERIALS

Fabric, 2m x 1.4m
(2¼yd x 56in)

☙

Piping

☙

Matching sewing thread

☙

Brushed cotton backing
fabric, 2m x 1.4m
(2¼yd x 56in)

☙

Thick wadding, 4m x 1.2m
(4½yd x 48in)

☙

Basting thread

STEP ONE

Lay the fabric down flat. Attaching piping to fabric is easier to do when the fabric is flat. An expert would pipe after quilting, but if you are a complete beginner the result will be more professional if you do it at this stage. Lay the piping down on the right side of the fabric so that the piping design faces into the main fabric, in this case the quilt. Pin the piping along the straight line in the fabric design or measure accurately from the selvedge edge to achieve a straight line.

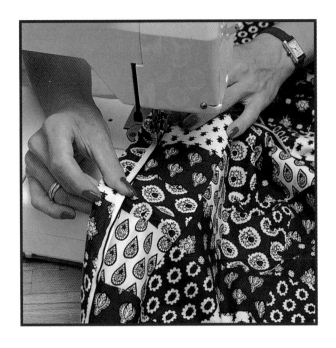

STEP TWO

Using a special foot on your sewing machine, which looks like one foot with two notches cut out of each side, lower the foot on to the decorative piping so that the needle is nearest the piping. Straight-stitch the piping in place along the length of the fabric.

STEP THREE

Assemble the layers for the quilt: backing fabric, wadding and piped top fabric. You might find that you cannot obtain a piece of wadding the exact size you require. If so, lay two pieces of wadding, which together equal the correct measurement, on a flat surface alongside one another and gently stitch them together with large cross stitches between the two. This will not increase the bulk of the wadding but will keep the two pieces together long enough until they are sandwiched by the fabric and held in place by the quilting.

STEP FOUR

Pin the backing fabric, wadding and top fabric together to secure. Then, using a curved needle to make large loops, baste the layers together with contrasting thread.

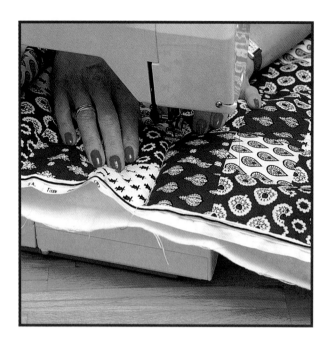

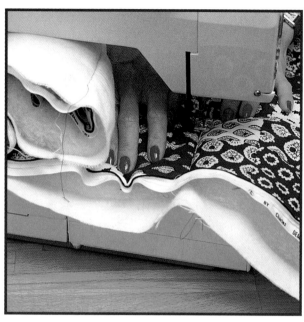

STEP FIVE

Using a sewing machine set on straight stitch, begin to stitch along the pattern lines of the fabric, feeding the thick sandwich of fabric beneath the looser machine tension. To prevent the fabric from buckling, work slowly using both hands to help.

STEP SIX

As you continue stitching along the quilt, the layers will become very bulky, particularly when you get to the middle. To deal with this, roll the stitched quilt quite firmly into a sausage of fabric, then continue as before. When you have completed the horizontal quilting, turn the fabric round and stitch down the length of the quilt, following the lines of the pattern as before. To finish the quilt, fold in the raw edges all the way around and hand-stitch in place.

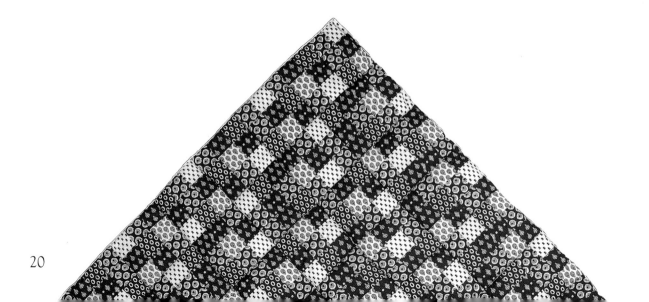

Wadding fabrics

There are many different products available worldwide for use in patchwork, quilting and appliqué and it can be difficult keeping abreast of the latest developments. Listed below are some of the main products that are readily available, together with their uses.

Transfer adhesive is a very thin layer of soft adhesive, like a webbed fabric, which is attached to greaseproof paper. It is ideal for appliqué work. Iron the transfer adhesive on to a fraying fabric with the paper attached. Then cut out the image to be appliquéd, peel off the paper backing and re-iron the image right side down on to your project (see the appliquéd towels on page 92).

Stiffened fabric pre-printed with a screen of 1cm (½in) blue squares is useful for patchwork. This can be used as a machine sewing guide to create geometric patterns and shapes, and would be ideal for a traditional pattern like the log cabin patchwork design.

Iron-on quilt wadding, which has diamond-shaped adhesive lines printed on soft interfacing, provides a stitched guide for accurate diamond-shaped quilting over patterned material.

Weights of wadding

Wadding fabrics for use in patchwork and quilting come in a range of five weights. They are all machine washable and can also be dry-cleaned.

The lightest iron-on wadding can be used for the most delicate of uses or just to give a thinner material more bulk and warmth. The iron-on wadding does not slip and is ideal for machine-quilting. The next weight up, a slightly thicker iron-on wadding, would give a stronger relief effect when quilted.

The middle-weight wadding is a compressed volume fleece; it is the same thickness as the previous weight but much warmer. The silk flower basket seen on page 40 is made with this wadding and the needle slips through it easily. The 1cm (½in) thick wadding can be used for lighter quilted covers, cushions or bulky clothing. The 4cm (1½in) thick wadding is the maximum weight I like sewing with using a household machine. It is bulky, warm and looks like a chunky quilt; this was used for all of the thick single bed quilts.

Appliqué

Soft-fleeced material is available in many colours for warm clothes lining or sporting clothes; it is easily washable, light and cosy. The new fleeced material is also excellent for patchwork and with applied appliqués in contrasting colours looks exceptionally effective. Another big discovery is polyester felt which comes in a wide range of colours and has the advantage of being washable; at my local shop it was less expensive than normal wool felt. I had previously made a blanket for my small daughter, after finally and with difficulty dispensing with her 'snugly', and as she grew I added blanket patches with more appliqué relevant to her life. As this fleece is so light it is ideal for the very young or very old, and rather good in between as well. Simple jackets, basic mittens or children's bonnets would also look good in fleece and blanket stitch.

Stitching effects

These fleece cushions are designed for my little boat and I can assure you that in England's often inhospitable waters, the warmer and cosier a cushion is, the happier the crew. With the nautical theme in mind, I designed small felt starfish, shells, fish and a flower and heart for fun. By varying the stitches, different effects and textures are achieved. Blanket stitch is used to bind the edge of a blanket to stop it fraying; it is a type of hemming for bulky materials. I have used blanket stitch to attach the fleece patches together, secure the small hearts in a row and, more traditionally, to edge the cushion, securing together the front and back cushion layers. Running stitch is another essential, running back and forth in any length. Very small running stitches are quite secure while looser ones are more decorative, like the wake that follows a boat or the water ripples from a fish. Running stitch is also used to secure the shell and as a double running stitch to create the border cuff around the cushion. French knots are used for the fish eyes, air bubbles and as filling for the centre of the pink and white daisies.

These brightly coloured fleecy cushions decorated with nautical appliqué motifs are extremely soft and cosy.

Making the cushions

As a small child, I made a gingham apron at school using all these very simple stitches, which I was very proud of at five years old. While these stitches are basic they are also very decorative, and extremely effective, whether you are attaching patches or securing appliqué. There are numerous other stitches you can use in appliqué; if you are interested in finding out more, I suggest you buy a stitch book which will demonstrate the versatility of embroidery stitching.

Polyester felt is an ideal fabric for use in appliqué, and worked especially well in this project. It is perfect for cutting out as it does not fray. When stitching felt in position, you do not need to turn under raw edges, and the needle slips through it easily. Look out for polyester felt that is washable and in a complete range of colours. I chose a range of basic colours that gave me pleasure and contrasted them with the vibrant pearl cotton threads. Choose any combination of colours and threads you prefer. These cushions are simple enough for young children to make – it would make a change from yet another gingham apron!

MATERIALS

Navy fleece, 1.4m x 70cm
(56in x 28in)

⟋⟍

Red fleece, 1.4m x 70cm
(56in x 28in)

⟋⟍

Selection of polyester felt
in assorted colours

⟋⟍

Sewing thread in
several colours

⟋⟍

2 cushion pads to fit

STEP ONE

Place the navy and red fleece together and cut out two side panels from opposite selvedge edges, one 70cm x 40cm (28in x 16in) and the other 70cm x 30cm (28in x 12in), for the cushion back. This will leave a 70cm x 70cm (28in x 28in) square in each colour fleece. Cut these squares into four pieces. Mix up the colours to give you perfectly matching but different-toned cushions. Using the templates on pages 26–7, cut out the appliqué images from polyester felt. To do this, pin the traced motif to the felt and then cut it out; the felt does not fray.

STEP TWO

Pin the felt hearts to a piece of navy fleece. Using contrasting coloured thread, blanket stitch the hearts in position. Keep the stitches even, and always loop the thread under the needle to form the blanket stitch.

STEP THREE

Continue to attach motifs to the pieces of fleece. How you position the appliqué images on the fleece pieces is up to you; you can place fishes with hearts or with boats and it does not matter. However, remember not to place any images too near to the border.

STEP FOUR

After attaching the appliqué motifs on one fleece patch, join two fleece patches together. To do this, blanket stitch down one fleece patch, then blanket stitch down the other fleece patch, but at each stitch pick up the top trailing stitch of the adjoining prestitched fleece patch. The two blanket stitch patches will then lie flat with the top loops of blanket stitch intertwined, joining them together.

STEP FIVE

Vary the stitches when adding appliqué motifs. Secure the shell to the fleece with small, neat overlapping stitches. Run the thread behind the fleece, then bring it up through the fleece and felt and neatly thread it back down beneath the fleece for the next stitch.

STEP SIX

Highlight the detail on the boat with small running stitches in a contrasting colour thread. Run the needle in and out, gathering a few stitches on the same needle. When you have stitched on all the appliqué motifs and joined all the patches, join the cushion front to the cushion back panels with blanket stitch along each edge. Change the colour of thread as you progress around the cushion.

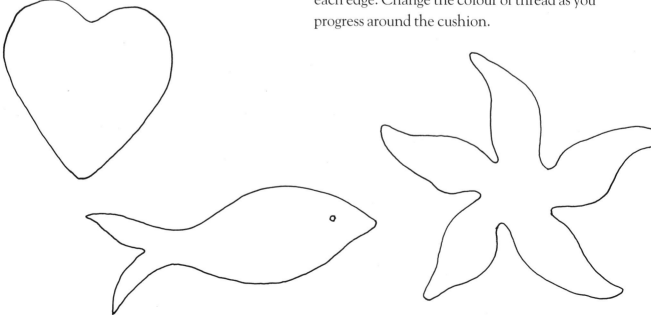

STEP SEVEN

Stitch a row of running stitches in contrasting thread 5cm (2in) in from the edge of the cushion to create a simple border.

STEP EIGHT

Add another row of running stitches 6mm (¼in) in from the first row all around the cushion to complete the border. This double running stitch duplicates the ripple of the fish and adds to the finished security of the cushion. When you have completed the cushion cover, insert a cushion pad through the flaps at the back.

$\backsim$ 1 $\backsim$
TODDLER'S QUILT

Children grow extremely quickly and their needs are constantly changing. Moving out of a cot and into their first bed is a big step. So this warm, washable and brightly coloured quilt is ideal for any small child, whether to snuggle under for an afternoon nap or to provide additional warmth during the winter. And it is not so big and cumbersome as to discourage a little person from making their bed!

Making the quilt

Choose the fabric for your quilt carefully. For those who want quick results, patchwork fabric is sold in larger fabric shops; some is stitched while some is printed to look like patchwork. Both types are ideal for quick and easy quilting projects. I finished this quilt in an afternoon! The thicker polyester wadding is both light and very warm for a small child; it is also, most importantly, safe and allergy-free. Gingham is another excellent choice of fabric for children; it looks clean and fresh even when well loved. It also has a timeless quality and can co-ordinate with many differing house styles and fabrics within a room. This quilt backing is made from a bold red gingham which contrasts with the smaller navy and white in the patchwork mix of natural and denim-coloured squares.

    The quilt was trimmed with a double use of different widths of ribbon. The wider, navy gathered ribbon offsets the red gingham, while the ruched, narrower red ribbon contrasts with the patchwork, and the small red ribbons scattered over the patchwork in the quilting tie the two together. This use of ribbon makes the quilt reversible. So, however apt the child is at folding the quilt, it will always look charming.

MATERIALS

Two pieces of fabric, each measuring 1.7m x 1.1m (68in x 44in)

೦೦

Polyester wadding, 1.7m x 1m (68in x 40in), 155g (5oz) weight

೦೦

Matching sewing thread

೦೦

Red ribbon, 4m (4½yd), 6mm (¼in) wide

೦೦

Red ribbon, 11m (12½yd), 1.5cm (⅝in) wide

೦೦

Navy ribbon, 11m (12½yd), 2.5cm (1in) wide

STEP ONE

Assemble the three layers of the quilt, sandwiching the polyester wadding between the fabrics of your choice. Select the area of patchwork squares you wish to distinguish in quilting and pin the layers together along these guidelines, working from the middle outwards. The individual squares of this patchwork would have been far too small to quilt, so I chose to quilt every third square.

STEP TWO

Using the sewing machine set on a loose tension, sew each pinned quilting guideline directly across the fabric width. As additional decoration, stitch 10cm (4in) bands of 6mm (¼in) contrasting red ribbon under the quilting stitch lines.

STEP THREE

As the quilting progresses, the completed quilt will become too bulky to work with. Roll the completed work into a sausage to allow you to progress comfortably with the machine. Then sew the quilt down the pinned fabric length to complete the quilted squares.

STEP FOUR

Trim the quilt with red pre-gathered ribbon next to the blue patchwork and an additional wider, navy gingham ribbon gathered by machine beneath it. Enclose the raw quilt edges against the wadding and pin the gathered wider blue gingham ribbon along the edge. Place the red ribbon uppermost on the quilted patchwork top. Stitch though all the layers together to finish the quilt.

2
BABY'S PUFF PATCHWORK QUILT

This patchwork quilt was made out of used summer clothing and a few remnants of differing pink gingham. Babies develop quickly so I wanted to make a quilt that could be used for carrying the baby in a nest, within the crib or for the bottom of the play pen. The individual puffs make it very light and exceptionally bouncy for the wobbly sitting-up stage when babies keep toppling over.

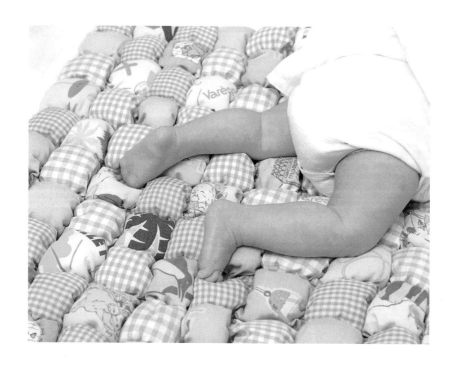

Making the quilt

This puff patchwork quilt in its pretty shades of pink is delightfully light, warm and cosy, whether it is used to cover the baby or to kick and gurgle on. The puff patches make the quilt extremely soft and bouncy. The quilted mattress and crib lining provide a safe and snug environment for a baby inside the crib, stopping any draughts and preventing small hands scratching against the wicker sides. They are both quick and easy projects to make and all the materials used to make them are very inexpensive and completely washable. Although there has recently been some safety controversy over babies' mattresses, rest assured that, if soiled, this mattress can easily go through the washing machine and tumble-drier and has nothing controversial within it.

The crib, which is made of traditional wicker, has a nostalgic quality and appeal, making it especially suitable for a patchwork quilt. The crib is light but very strong and excellent for growing babies and their siblings who want to participate in their upbringing. I had the crib made especially with the higher hood for this reason; the hood also protects against draughts and enthusiastic tumbling children.

MATERIALS

Gingham fabric, 156cm x 78cm (62⅜in x 31¼in)

❧

Patterned fabric, 156cm x 78cm (62⅜in x 31¼in)

❧

Cardboard packaging

❧

Matching sewing thread

❧

Polyester wadding, 84cm x 84cm (33½in x 33½in), 155g (5oz) weight

❧

White piqué fabric for backing, 1m x 1m (40in x 40in)

STEP ONE

Using the two outer squares on page 105, make a cardboard window template. To cut out a patch, place the template on the fabric and, using a pencil, mark the fabric around the outside and the inside of the template. Cut along the outer pencilled square; the inner pencilled square is the sewing line. Cut out 72 patches from both fabrics in this way.

Pin a row of 12 patches together, alternating the fabrics, by lining up the pins through the inner pencilled squares on each patch. Machine-stitch along the pinned lines. Join the 12 rows together in the same way.

STEP TWO

Using a sewing machine, gather over the patchwork joins, reducing it to gathered patches measuring 6cm (2⅜in). Cut out 144 polyester wadding squares, each measuring 6cm (2⅜in).

Lay the backing fabric down flat. Leaving a 15cm (6in) border, divide the fabric with pins into 144 squares measuring 6cm (2¾in).

Lay the patchwork on top and attach the first gathered row to the row of pins beneath. For patch 1, pin-pierce through the outer edge of the patchwork to the first pin marker. Pin between patches 1 and 2 to the second marker. Pin between patches 2 and 3 to the third marker and continue to the end of the row. Machine-stitch down the right side of the patchwork to attach it to the backing fabric. Place a square of wadding into each of the first row gathered. Pin and stitch row 2 in the same way. Be careful not to leave pins within the quilt.

When you have finished one side of the quilt, machine-stitch down the other side of the patches to enclose the wadding.

STEP THREE

To finish the puff patchwork quilt, cut a sausage roll of wadding for each side of the quilt. Place it on the backing fabric border adjacent to the puff quilt and roll over the 15cm (6in) border to encase the wadding. Hand-stitch the border down.

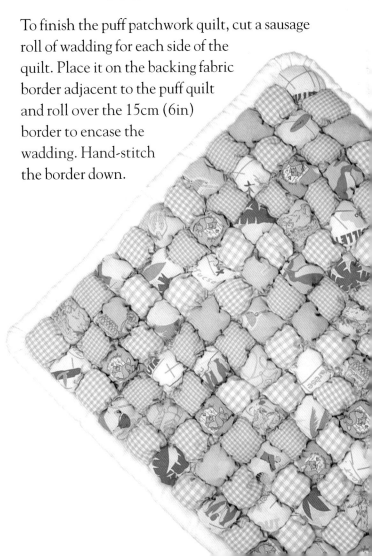

$\mathcal{M}$aking the crib lining and mattress

Any mother will want her baby to be comfortable, warm, protected from draughts and entirely snug. So, anything made for a baby should be made from non-controversial material, and be durable, washable, light and pretty. This simple crib lining fulfils all these criteria, plus it is inexpensive to make from cotton sheeting and washable polyester wadding. The mattress is also quick and easy to make and will add a charming finishing touch to this traditional wicker crib. Choose white cotton sheeting for simplicity, and any colour of perlé cotton for the quilting and frill edging.

MATERIALS

Cotton sheeting

⟲

Matching sewing thread

⟲

Polyester wadding,
155g (5oz) weight,
for the mattress

⟲

Contrasting perlé cotton

⟲

Polyester wadding,
75g (2½oz) weight,
for the crib lining

Made to fit a traditional wicker crib, this pretty quilted lining and mattress provide a snug and cosy environment for a baby.

STEP ONE

Place cotton sheeting into the base of the crib and pin out the semi oval form of the mattress. Place the fabric on a flat surface and cut out two mattress forms, allowing a 2cm (¾in) seam allowance. With right sides facing, machine-stitch the two mattress pieces around the edges, taking a 1.5cm (⅝in) seam allowance and leaving a 20cm (8in) opening gap. Turn the mattress sheeting the right way out, enclosing the seam inside.

Cut two layers of polyester wadding the same size as the mattress form. Place the wadding within the stitched mattress sheeting. Free hand-quilt the mattress by making small stitches in contrasting perlé cotton thread; overstitch twice and tie the knot at the back. Slipstitch the mattress sheeting closed. Try not to use pins in case you forget one; if you must use them, however, count out ten and then count back ten!

STEP TWO

To make the crib lining, place cotton sheeting into the crib to pin out a rough shape. Replace the pattern sheet, and make two small darts to accommodate the curve of the hood. Machine-stitch the darts. Cut a second pattern for the foot of the crib and make darts for this too. Cut a length of overstitched double frill of cotton sheeting for the trim and gather the edges.

Place the right sides of the crib lining together; place the trim with the overstitched edge facing inwards between the crib lining pieces around the curved edge. Machine-stitch around the edge. Turn the crib lining right side out. Repeat to trim the lining for the foot of the crib.

Cut out a piece of wadding to fit the lining and place it between the layers of sheeting, cutting an inverted V for the dart. Slipstitch the lining closed. Free hand-quilt the lining with contrasting coloured perlé cotton; make double stitches and tie them with a jaunty knot. Quilt the lining for the foot of the crib in the same way.

3
HAND-QUILTED CUSHIONS

Quilting is a method of sandwiching fabrics together to create warmth and durability and to extend the life of the fabric. At one time, many household items were quilted, including bed covers, cushions, baby items, underclothing, men's waistcoats and women's bodices. These were often embellished with decorative hems, cuffs and collars, while quilted wedding garments were decorated with beautiful stitched details.

Quilting designs

Hand-quilting was both a practical and ornate craft and it is frequently seen on smooth polished cloths, such as silk and cotton; because of the stitching work involved, the fabric tends to be of good quality. The old quilts that I adore are often plain silk on one side and a cotton floral for the backing, to stop the quilt sliding off the bed. Many of the older designs are in the stylized form of roses, shells or leaves, with lovely geometric trellis or square patterns. The designs fill the whole quilted area, forming swirls of stitched movement which show distinctively on the silk while secretly weaving paths among the floral motif on the backing.

Do look at older quilts for design inspirations and local motifs and incorporate them into your quilting designs. Many designs can now be adapted to quilting and often simpler ones are the most effective. Stencil designs work exceptionally well as they are naturally created in a series of lakes and bridges which also work for the quilting technique.

Flowers and fruit are traditional designs used in quilting.

I carefully designed the Turk's head rope pattern for the red cushion, which is clever and works well. Then, on picking up one of my old stencil designs of flowers and fruit, I found that this worked equally well, so I used this design for the white cushion. This stencil looks charming when quilted and has a refinement that the other, busier design lacks. Look around for quilting examples for inspiration. Although most are machine created, they could be quilted by hand. Enlarge or reduce designs on a photocopier to suit the space you need to quilt.

I tried using the iron-on wadding (see page 21) for hand-quilting, and I must admit to not being very satisfied with the results, although I found it ideal for machine quilting. So much of sewing is personal preference so do experiment to find the method that suits you best.

Turk's head rope design

The template for the Turk's head rope quilting design is composed of four sections.

The red cushion pattern is taken from the Turk's head rope design (see template above) which can be laid flat or pulled up in a button; the rope forms a wonderful moving, round pattern. The whole design is used on the red cushion but, if you prefer, separate elements could be used, such as a single rope quilted across a cushion or several ropes intertwined and repeating as you place them at will.

To make the Turk's head rope design, enlarge the template to a size suitable for you, and cut away the excess blank paper from the rope outline. You will see that the design is composed of four sections. Trace out the rope outline directly on to silk. Repeat for each of the four outline sections; in this way you will not lose the swirl of the design. Quilt as before, following the individual movement of each rope curve, then thread the needle back through the wadding to commence the next rope curve. This design is an unusual and interesting design to quilt.

Quilting the cushion

Quilting can be quite daunting to a newcomer. I remember being so intimidated by all the frames and ribbons stretching out pieces of shiny silk that I did not try the technique for ages, thinking it far too complicated. Many of the traditional methods of quilting are exceptionally time consuming but, however, I found that they are not always necessary, and I recommend that you cheat as much as possible!

This cushion design is very easy to quilt as long as you remember to follow the natural curves of the design when stitching. Make a long false stitch back between the wadding and backing when you have finished one element of the design and need to transfer to the next, for example when you have finished one grape and are going on to the next. In this design, the grapes fall from the trellis basket with abundance while the heavier peaches or apples add a stabilizing force to the vine leaves extending out into the silk. If you think the design is too busy and would prefer a simpler, more open pattern, feel free to adapt the design to suit your cushion, by repeating or pruning leaves or fruit from the quilt design, as required. Once you have practised with this design, you can go on to quilt your own patterns.

MATERIALS

Two pieces of silk for cushion cover, each 40cm x 40cm (16in x 16in)

∞

Cotton sheeting for backing, 40cm x 40cm (16in x 16in)

∞

Compressed volume fleece, 40cm x 40cm (16in x 16in)

∞

Lightweight wadding 40cm x 40cm (16in x 16in)

∞

Matching sewing thread

∞

Cushion pad, 40cm x 40cm (16in x 16in)

STEP ONE

Remove the fruit and flowers template from page 107 and enlarge if desired. Then trace over the back of the design with a soft pencil, either 2B or 3B. Lay the tracing, pencil side down, on top of one square of ironed silk. Secure the tracing in place with masking tape. Using a slightly harder pencil, such as an HB, go over the design outlines. Keep lifting up the paper as you go to check that the design has transferred on to the silk.

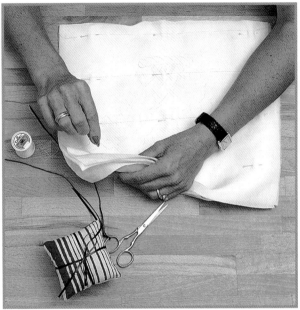

STEP TWO

When you have finished going over the lines, remove the tracing. If any of the lines are not very clear, go over them with the HB pencil. The marks have to be just good enough for you to see, but not too strong. You can refer back to your design if the lines become faint while you are working.

STEP THREE

Assemble the following four layers of fabric: the cotton sheeting backing, a compressed volume fleece, a square of wadding, and finally the silk. Pin the layers together at equal intervals. Then baste the quilt sandwich into 5cm (2in) squares (for a larger-sized quilt the basting would be further apart).

STEP FOUR

Using a light needle, quilt with running stitch along the traced lines on the silk, taking the thread through all four layers of fabric. To do this, gather three or four stitches on to the needle at a time and then pull it through the fabric. Use your fingers underneath the layers to guide the needle back in an equal stitch motion. When you have finished, make up the cushion cover by stitching a square of silk to the front of the quilted silk, right sides facing, leaving a gap. Turn the cover right side out, insert the cushion pad and slipstitch the gap to close.

4
QUILTED GIFTS

Quilting can be used over coat hangers, around the top of work baskets, or for pincushions or needleholders, all of which make ideal gifts. They are quick to stitch, and make practical and charming additions to the home. These items do not require much fabric; you can even use up small pieces of material left over from other projects.

Making a padded coat hanger

When you have a cramped wardrobe like mine, padded coat hangers can help to separate hanging clothes, thereby avoiding unsightly creases. They are also an excellent way to avoid the 'hanger look' for woollens, as well as protecting delicate silks and sheer fabrics. But even if you do not have an overcrowded wardrobe, padded coat hangers can be extremely pretty accessories in a bedroom!

You can use any sort of wooden coat hanger for this project. Indeed it is a good way of brightening up those old, chipped coat hangers that can be found in most wardrobes. You could also use wire or plastic coat hangers, although you will need more wadding and fabric to cover them. Use any suitable offcuts of fabric you have in your sewing basket – you do not need much to cover one hanger. Choose fabrics with small patterns, such as twining flowers, simple stripes or coloured dots, rather than fabrics with large, bold designs which would not be obvious on such a small scale as on a hanger. Alternatively, you could buy a selection of remnant fabrics from a haberdasher's, and then cover a whole batch of coat hangers to make perfect Christmas presents for all the family!

MATERIALS

Wooden coat hanger

૭౨

Bias binding

૭౨

Sticky tape or glue

૭౨

Wadding, 50cm (20in),
70g (2½oz) in weight

૭౨

Cotton fabric,
65cm x 15cm (26in x 6in)

૭౨

Matching sewing thread

૭౨

Ribbon or lace to trim

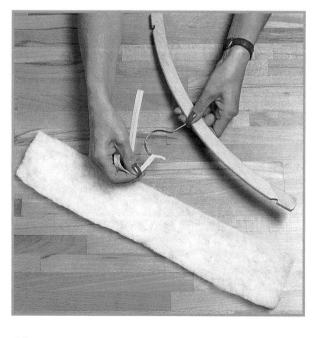

STEP ONE

Wrap bias binding around the tip of the metal hook of the hanger and secure with sticky tape or a spot of glue. Then, holding the binding firmly in position, slowly rotate the hanger. The descending spiral of binding will cover the metal hook completely. Secure the end of the binding to the wooden hanger with tape or glue.

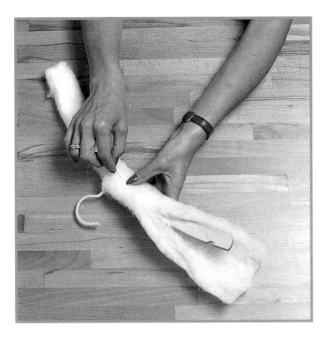

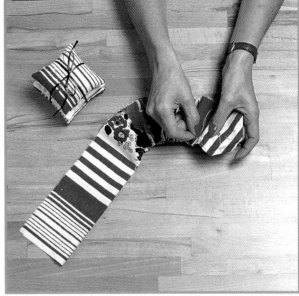

STEP TWO

Cut a strip of wadding to fit around the wooden part of the hanger, allowing extra to cover the ends. Wrap the wadding around the hanger and fold in the ends. Secure the wadding firmly in position with tacking.

STEP THREE

Measure the length and width of the padded hanger. To calculate the amount of fabric required, add a third to both measurements to allow for gathering, then double the width to allow for covering both sides of the hanger. Cut out the fabric strip. Fold the fabric in half lengthwise with the wrong sides of the strip together. Pin the ends and gather the strip by hand along the folded edge and at the ends.

STEP FOUR

Slip the gathered fabric over the padded hanger, and stitch the top edges of the fabric together enclosing the hanger. Continue to gather the fabric along the length of the hanger. When you have finished the gathering, distribute the gathers evenly and secure the thread. Tie a pretty ribbon or strip of lace around the hanger hook to complete.

Quick quilting ideas

The lined basket with its padded rim makes a perfect work basket, being both smart enough to be left in the sitting room and orderly enough to house your sewing tools. I frequently use the padded edge as a pincushion while working on projects, while small articles of sewing can be tucked neatly out of view, protected from the basketwork by the fabric lining.

Smaller offcuts of fabric can be made into charming pincushions. When stacked and tied with a bow they make excellent presents, being festive, practical and pretty.

The small, slightly padded needleholder made from the rose motif within the fabric helps me define my needle's weight, length and usage better than when storing needles within the pincushions. Needles often disappear beneath wadding, only to give a sharp reminder on their reappearance weeks later through the other side.

Stack of pincushions

This stack of pincushions is made from three rectangles of fabric, each measuring 18 x 9cm (7¼ x 3½ in). Select fabrics with different pattern combinations, perhaps with stripes running in different directions. Or you could make the little stack in plain fabrics – a pile of pastel pincushions or a wild combination of bright colours would look very contemporary. Hunt through scraps of leftover material in your workbasket that you could use, as so little is needed. To make each pincushion, fold the fabric in half and machine-stitch around two sides, leaving the third free. Turn the pincushion right side out. Stuff an 8cm (3¼ in) thick wedge of polyester wadding in the interior pocket, then add a 7cm (2¾ in) square on top to make the little pincushion very plump. Slipstitch along the fourth side to complete. Make three pincushions and stack them together with a ribbon.

Needleholder

This is another gift that can be made from a scrap of fabric. Needleholders are an encouragement to grade my needles correctly and to store them flat, enabling me to select not only the eye, but the needle length and point.

To make the needleholder, cut a large flower from a piece of fabric leaving a slight border for the hem. Cut another piece of fabric for the backing. Place the flower right side down on the backing and machine-stitch around the edge of the flower using the reverse image on the back of the fabric as a guide. Leave a 3cm (1¼ in) gap in the stitching and cut tiny notches all around the outside of the flower. Turn the needleholder right side out, pad the interior with a thin wadding, enclose a length of ribbon and slipstitch the gap to close.

Lined workbasket

Lay the lining fabric into the basket and fit the base, then the sides; a large triangular excess of material will be left at each corner. Pin these fabric triangles to the lining to fit the basket. Machine down each of the four corner-pinned darts. Gather a contrasting material and stitch this to the raw edge of the lining, leaving a gap for the handle on each side. Stitch or glue wadding over the edge of the basket. Place the basket lining in the basket so that the edges overlap the wadding. Gather the edge with a strand of perlé cotton.

49

❧ 5 ❧
GEOMETRIC PATCHWORK CUSHIONS

Patchwork is ideal for creating your own designs, combining colours and patterns, and using the pattern directions to add additional intrigue to your work. Each of these four cushions was created with the aim of using them on my new little boat, so a traditional patchwork design of the compass was used, with a little artistic licence.

Making the compass cushion

The compass patchwork cushions were not difficult to design and I would encourage anyone to have a go at designing their own. The difficult part was sewing the right part of the pattern together. I made so many mistakes while chatting to the children or half-watching television that, after all my unpicking, I decided to use the template more carefully, and arranged the patchwork pieces in perfect order for the next one to be joined, to avoid any more unpicking! A wonderful pile of small-patterned, blue and white fabrics inspired these cushions. The varied tones give excellent scope to play with the *trompe-l'oeil* movement of the cushions, as they can change in perspective as you walk around the room.

When designing the compass patchwork I did join many patchwork points into the middle of the cushion, despite advice to the contrary, and found that the cushions worked very well, but I would suggest steering clear of creating a design where more than 16 points meet!

Each cushion is edged with a broad mount, adding to the finished effect. As the cushions are hand-stitched, I backed the patchwork with sheeting before stitching on the cushion backs in the usual way. The backing sheet will give the cushions additional strength, enabling them to bear the strain of many a jeaned bottom as my children flop down on the tender stitches!

MATERIALS

Six blue and white fabrics of your choice, all 90cm x 30cm (36in x 12in)

၆၅

Matching sewing thread

၆၅

Cotton sheeting, 45cm x 45cm (18in x 18in)

၆၅

Fabric for cushion back, 45cm x 45cm (18in x 18in)

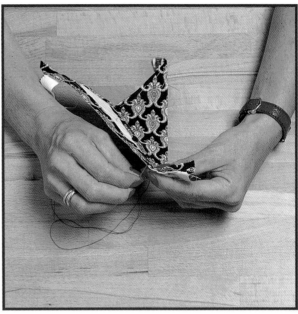

STEP ONE

Cut out the patchwork pieces, using any of the templates featured on pages 97–103, enlarged by 111 per cent, and baste these to the paper templates, as shown on page 13. Place the patches on to the master template, covering a quarter of the cushion at a time in order to check placement.

STEP TWO

Begin to sew the pattern pieces together in the correct order. Place one patch against another, with right sides together, and pin the tips together to avoid slippage. Oversew along one side, stitching as closely and firmly as possible.

STEP THREE

Continue stitching the patches together until you have completed the compass design. Then stitch the borders and corner triangles in position so that you have a square shape. Finally, stitch the borders around the compass design (see page 14) and complete the cushion as shown on page 62.

6
TUMBLING BLOCKS TABLECLOTH

The traditional tumbling blocks pattern is one of my favourite patchwork designs. There are many exceptional examples of quilts made in this design, using the darkest silks to floral baby cottons. This design is frequently used to make a baby's first patchwork quilt and I have always admired the soft colours used in this type of patchwork. I chose to make this tablecloth from men's shirts in order to retain the soft colours of a baby's quilt but also to create a crisp cloth cover for a round table.

Making the tablecloth

Many potential quilt designs can be seen in our everyday environment, such as ceramic flooring and tiled walls in hexagons, diamonds and squares. Cubes, blocks and rhomboids are all excellent geometric shapes for patchwork designs. For inspiration, look particularly at corner details in large or old buildings and sketch or photograph them so you can then transform them into your next creation. New ideas translated from older designs are a tribute to good design.

This patchwork is made entirely from men's shirts, all of which have been worn! Many brave fellows contributed, so my tablecloth contains a wonderful record of my son, father, brothers and friends, and the shirts combine to form a fresh three-dimensional look on life.

Cutting patches

The tablecloth measures 2m (80in) square and is made up of several hundred cubes, each of which is made from three pieces, so you will need to cut plenty of templates and pieces of fabric. The cost of the whole patchwork was the price of one single flat cotton sheet, basting thread and strong sewing thread, which I consider quite inexpensive for such a beautiful result. You must have patience however; this patchwork took me a whole summer to stitch.

The first thing to do is to collect together as many shirts as you can; many of my shirts arrived halfway through making the quilt. In order to begin, I worked on smaller areas and joined them later to form larger patchwork areas. Cut up the shirts, discarding seams, collars, cuffs and yoke, and then iron each piece well and check for additional wear on elbows or stains down the front.

Place the cut patches into categories of dark, medium and light. For the light category I used white throughout. My family mainly wore blue or white shirts. However, a Norwegian friend gave me two very dashing shirts, one of which was deep blue with red and white lines running through the fabric. I cut this shirt in two ways: one set of patches had two stripes while the other had one. Look out for different possibilities in your fabric selections.

MATERIALS

Cotton fabric, 2m x 2m
(2¼yd x 2¼yd), or about
25 old shirts

❧

Basting thread

❧

Matching sewing thread

❧

Single white cotton sheet

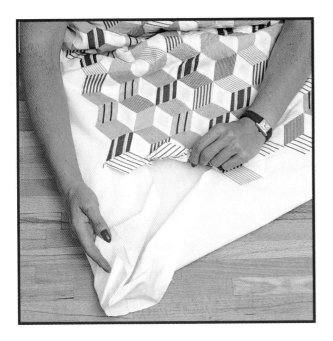

STEP ONE

Using the template on page 105, cut out the patches, following the direction of nap and pattern. Stitch the patches together in cubes (see page 14) with a dark patch on the left, a medium one on the right and a light patch across the top. Oversew the blocks together to make the tablecloth. Lay a cotton sheet on a flat surface. Place the patchwork on top. Fold back the sheet edges under the patchwork so that there is a 10cm (4in) border around the edge. Pin, then baste to secure. Hand-stitch the patchwork to the sheet backing along the straight edges of the cover. Fold each corner of the sheet back beneath the patchwork.

STEP TWO

Smooth out the fold to form a perfect, 45° mitred corner. If preferred, you can cut away the excess fabric. I left the folded material to give more substance and weight to the corner which is likely to become worn first. Stitch the mitred corner with tiny slipstitches. To quilt the patchwork, select occasional patchwork blocks and hand-quilt each patch individually with running stitch to connect the patchwork to the backing (see page 43).

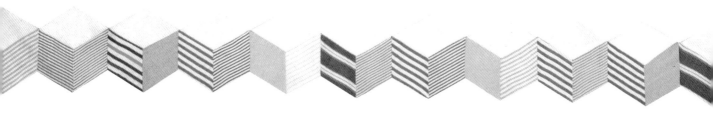

∽ 7 ∽
SILK PATCHWORK CUSHIONS

Both of these colourful patchwork cushion designs come, curiously enough, from parquet flooring patterns. An American friend dragged me out of my studio into the bright summer's light one day to visit a few cathedrals. It was there that I rediscovered stained glass. As a result, the parquet flooring outlines became filled with the jewel-like colours from the stained glass and these patchwork cushions are the result.

Making a patchwork cushion panel

I had odd remnants of silk in my work basket but they did not do justice to the patchwork design, so I went out on a silk hunt and found this pre-quilted jewel-like silk. The ivory silk works well as a cushion backing for the patchwork of men's ties, as do the navy, red, purple and green on the larger cushion. The thickness of the quilted fabric is not a problem with the little patch templates. The machine-quilted lines within the silk add to the direction of each patch, accentuating the *trompe-l'oeil* dimension of the patchwork cushions.

MATERIALS

Four colours of quilted silk, each measuring 90cm x 20cm (36in x 8in)

৩৩

Basting thread

৩৩

Matching sewing thread

STEP ONE

Enlarge the template on page 109 by 111 per cent, then photocopy it; or use the one on page 111 if you prefer. I used the first design five times for a 45cm x 45cm (18in x 18in) cushion. The template is small and could prove fiddly if this is your first attempt at patchwork. You might like to enlarge the design further on to A3 paper. Cut out the photocopied templates along the outlines into the individual template patches.

STEP TWO

Lay the paper templates on to the selected fabrics. Although the pattern templates appear to be the same, their position is different on the silk slub. When working on all other materials, the patterns must be placed following the nap or pattern, as this position enhances the *trompe-l'oeil* three-dimensional effect. Place the little square in a diamond position and the larger square squarely over the slub.

STEP THREE

Cut out the patches, leaving a 6mm (¼in) turning. Fold back the turning on to the paper pattern on each patch. Baste the turnings on to the patches firmly and accurately.

STEP FOUR

Place the patches on a spare template (see page 14) to avoid misplacing them. It is very easy to make mistakes with this design, especially with plain fabrics where the slub is the only guide. Stitch the silk patches together one by one by placing them right sides together and oversewing with whipping stitch.

STEP FIVE

When you have completed the patchwork, remove the basting stitches and carefully pull out the paper templates. Make up the cushion cover by following the instructions on page 62.

Making a flap-over cushion

These flap-over cushion covers are quick and easy to make; you can use this method for cotton pillows or silk cushions. Alter the measurements to suit your requirements, keeping a large or small Oxford cuff (border) or even none at all.

MATERIALS

Cushion pad, 45cm x 45cm
(18in x 18in)

෨

Quilted silk fabric,
1m x 45cm (40in x 18in)

෨

Matching sewing thread

STEP ONE

Lay the quilted silk fabric down flat. Place the patchwork panel in the middle of this strip of fabric to check the positioning. Pin in place.

STEP TWO

Fold under and hem the raw short edges of the quilted silk. Then hem the patchwork to the silk, turning under any rough edges, so that the patchwork forms a neat square.

STEP THREE

Fold in both hemmed edges of the cushion cover so that they overlap over the patchwork. Pin, then machine-stitch together the front and back side edges, taking a 1.5cm (⅝in) seam allowance. Turn the cushion cover the right way out through the central flap.

STEP FOUR

Machine around the edge of the patchwork to create the Oxford cuff (border around the cushion). You could alternatively use wide over-stitching for a more decorative effect. Insert the cushion pad through the cushion flap to complete.

~8~
SILK AND VELVET PATCHWORK THROW

A patchwork throw, especially if made from squares of silk and velvet, can be light and warm and is ideal for draping around the shoulders or wrapping over the knees on a cool evening. The additional detailing of small beads between each patch and trailing black cord tassels adorning each corner adds to the exotic feeling. This throw is a glorious addition both to a room and to evening comfort.

Making the throw

The choice of fabrics for this throw was made quite by accident. While I was buying the silk for the *trompe-l'oeil* cushions (see page 58), my eye was caught by a remnant of dazzling embroidered Indian silk, which I could not resist. I then found an even smaller piece of the same fabric and so I bought both pieces, which together came to just over 1m (40in) of fabric. One of the advantages of patchwork is collecting remnants – the size of the pieces does not matter as they are going to be cut up anyway!

I decided to use this fabric to make a patchwork throw, and partnered the lustrous silk with squares of soft black velvet to make a stunning combination, and a perfect example that patchwork does not have to be restricted to homespun fabrics!

Combining different textures and weights of fabric like the silk and velvet can be very effective; with both fabrics having lustrous finishes the overall effect is sumptuous and soft. Recently, I combined patches of Harris tweed and linen to make a new cover for a country footstool and cushion. Again, these two unlikely combinations were extremely effective, proving that patchwork can add allure and charm inexpensively.

MATERIALS

Silk fabric, 1m x 90m
(40in x 36in)

೬೦

Velvet, 1m x 90cm
(40in x 36in)

೬೦

Matching sewing thread

೬೦

Matching backing fabric,
2m x 90cm (80in x 36in)

೬೦

4 cord tassels

೬೦

100 black beads

STEP ONE

Using the square template on page 105, cut out a stiff cardboard template to match. Cut out a pile of patches in both materials and, using the cardboard template as a guide, mark two opposite sides of each patch with tailor's chalk. This is the stitching line.

STEP TWO

With right sides facing, pin alternate fabric squares together to make a row of patches. Insert the pin through the line of tailor's chalk on the first patch, and then through the chalk line on the adjoining patch.

STEP THREE

Machine-stitch the row of patches, stitching along the chalked lines. Remove the pins. Join the next row of patches in the same way, but alternating the fabric patches; if you started the first row with silk followed by velvet, start the next row with velvet followed by silk, and so on. Stitch all the rows in this way, alternating the fabric patches as you go.

STEP FOUR

Place the rows on a flat surface, to ensure that the patches alternate. To join one row to the adjacent one, replace the template on the attached patch row and align a ruler with the top of it. Use this to mark the stitching line along the entire row with tailor's chalk. This method is foolproof. Machine-stitch along the marked lines to join all the rows together.

STEP FIVE

Stitch a cord tassel to each corner of the throw, on the right side of the fabric. Cut a piece of backing fabric to fit the throw. With right sides together, machine-stitch the backing to the throw around all four sides, taking a 1.5cm (⅝in) seam allowance and sandwiching the tassels between the throw and the backing. Leave a small opening on one side.

STEP SIX

Turn the throw the right way out and slipstitch the opening. Pin the throw to the backing at points throughout the patchwork and stitch a small pillar of black beads to the throw at each intersection of patches. To do this, make a couple of stitches in the throw to secure the thread, then thread two or three beads on to the needle and a final baby bead. Then double the thread back down the first few beads (not the baby bead) to the backing and secure with a few small stitches.

There are so many beautiful trimmings you can use with patchwork. I am tempted to go and find fabrics just to tone with these wonderful tassels.

9
MIXED MEDIA APPLIQUED BED LINEN

Decorate your bed linen with a marvellous mixture of colours, fabrics, pastel crayons, felt-tip pens, free machine embroidery, zigzag stitch and other machine stitches to create a truly original night-time retreat. Make your duvet cover as pretty as you like, or cover it with inspirational and personal mementos for a unique decoration.

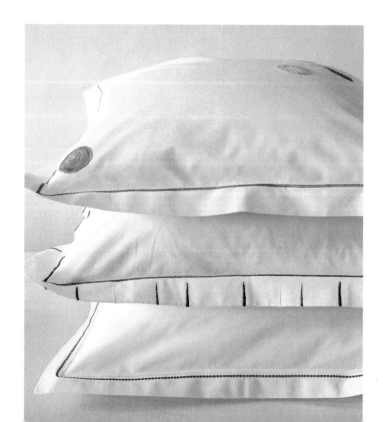

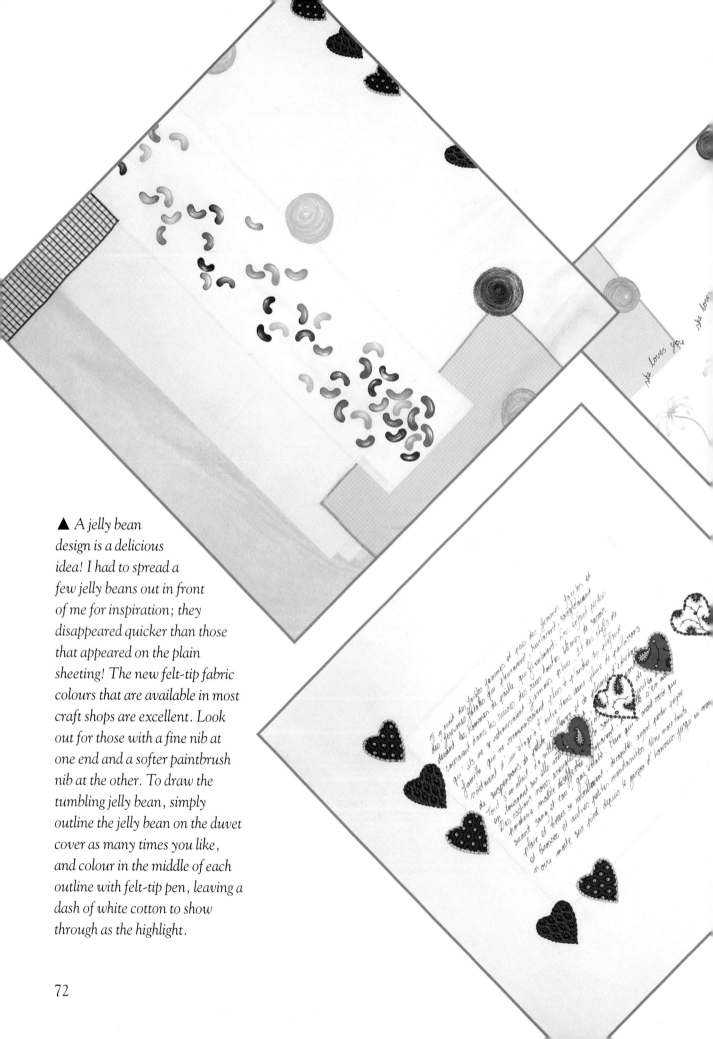

▲ A jelly bean
design is a delicious
idea! I had to spread a
few jelly beans out in front
of me for inspiration; they
disappeared quicker than those
that appeared on the plain
sheeting! The new felt-tip fabric
colours that are available in most
craft shops are excellent. Look
out for those with a fine nib at
one end and a softer paintbrush
nib at the other. To draw the
tumbling jelly bean, simply
outline the jelly bean on the duvet
cover as many times you like,
and colour in the middle of each
outline with felt-tip pen, leaving a
dash of white cotton to show
through as the highlight.

72

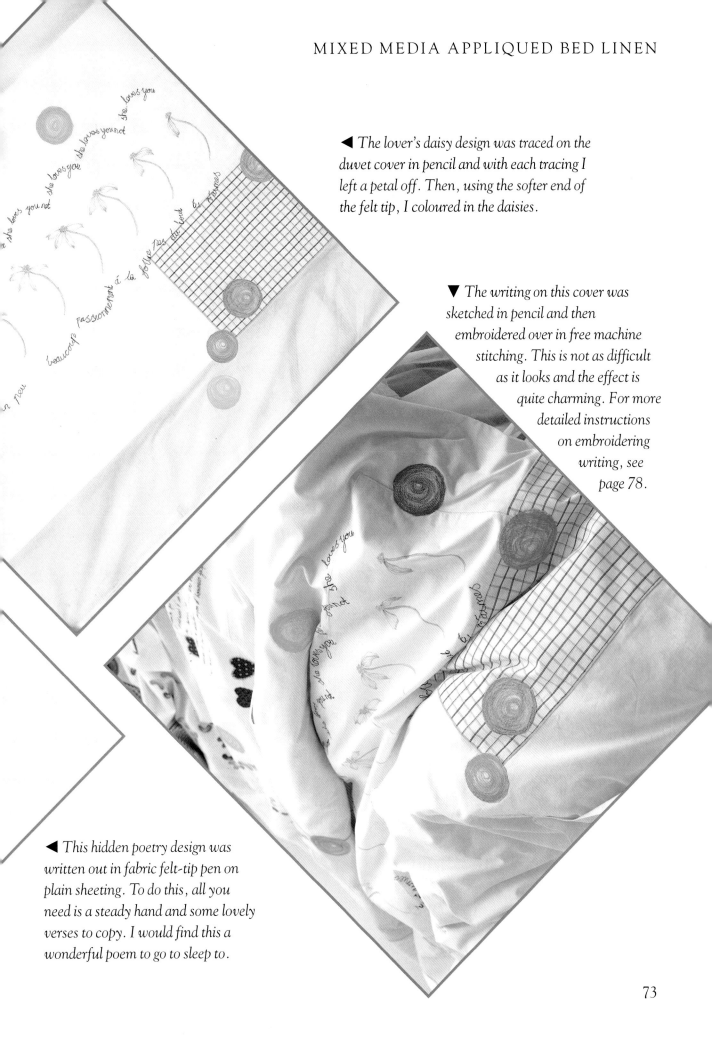

◀ *The lover's daisy design was traced on the duvet cover in pencil and with each tracing I left a petal off. Then, using the softer end of the felt tip, I coloured in the daisies.*

▼ *The writing on this cover was sketched in pencil and then embroidered over in free machine stitching. This is not as difficult as it looks and the effect is quite charming. For more detailed instructions on embroidering writing, see page 78.*

◀ *This hidden poetry design was written out in fabric felt-tip pen on plain sheeting. To do this, all you need is a steady hand and some lovely verses to copy. I would find this a wonderful poem to go to sleep to.*

Decorating bed linen

Here, large patches of checked shirt material were appliquéd to the duvet cover, with pastel crayon appliqué bubbles dancing and floating, linking one area to other. Poetry written in fabric felt-tip pen hides its elusive verses behind fabric hearts appliquéd with decorative machine stitching. Jelly beans tumble down a plain white panel in vibrant, jostling felt-tip colours. A delicate daisy has plucked petals to test a lover's thoughts in softly used fabric felt-tips; there is English verse above and French beneath, both coming to different conclusions.

The pillow cases are similarly embellished, with decorative stitching on one, flashes of machine stitching on another and appliquéd pastel crayon bubbles on the third. With such pretty decoration, this is a wonderful bed to creep into for sweet dreams!

Crayons and pastels are so easy to use, you could write out nursery rhymes for the very young and together with the child draw a cat, dog and chickens, or stick-legged cows and curly wool sheep. Older children might like cartoons, and perhaps some helpful hints on tidying their bedrooms! Choose motifs relevant to the pillow's user to make the bed linen truly personalized.

MATERIALS

White cotton sheeting

Duvet cover

Pillowcases

Sewing thread

STEP ONE

Using fabric pastel pens, make a circular doodle in each colour on plain cotton sheeting. If desired, colour over the doodle with the pen further to achieve more depth of colour.

STEP TWO

Cut out the coloured pastel bubbles. Snip out small wedges of fabric around the edge of each circle to accommodate the curve when the raw edge is folded underneath in Step 3.

STEP THREE

Fold under the raw edges of each bubble and baste them down on the reverse of the coloured side to give a neat, circular edge to the bubbles.

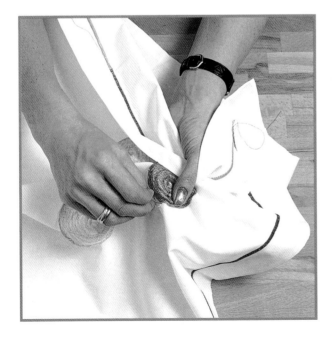

STEP FOUR

Position the coloured pastel bubbles randomly on the bed linen and pin in place. Hand-stitch them to the linen using neat hemming stitches.

~10~
STITCH-APPLIQUED TEA TOWELS

The first thing I think about each morning when I get up is coffee. And now that I have even designed coffee cups on my drying-up towels, I must be more addicted than I thought! I find it fun to decorate towels and other linen with personal details; instead of china coffee cups, you could embroider motifs from your favourite sporting activity, a special holiday or a memorable occasion.

Stitching the towels

Free machine stitching gives an easy, sketched look with threads on fabric and it can be used on all sorts of items. Free machine stitching is, as its name suggests, quite free, so when following a line the stitching will always be fluid.

Sketching my coffee cups and searching through my Italian dictionary gave me inspiration for this design. To put together your motif, trace over fabric patterns, magazine pictures and any text that you like; then sketch them out on to your fabric and begin stitching.

MATERIALS

Tea towels

Sewing thread in
varying colours

due caffè

uno cappuccino

tre espressi

STEP ONE

Using the template above, sketch out the design on the tea towel. If the fabric has an open weave, simply place the towel over the template and sketch it on the fabric. If the fabric has a close weave, trace the design first, then transfer the tracing on to the fabric. Make sure that any words are readable and are not mirror images.

STEP TWO

Place the towel in an embroidery hoop so that the fabric is on the lower stretch, that is the opposite to embroidery. Prepare the sewing machine for free embroidery. Tilt the hoop underneath the needle if the needle clearance is not high enough.

STEP THREE

Using coloured sewing thread, embroider the tea towel, following the pencil outlines for guidance. If you have never free machine-stitched before, you will find that it is an odd sensation. Keep the hoop flat and hold a finger over the loose thread end to begin with, then stitch at a moderate pace. Try differing stitches, such as zigzag and running stitch, and try a shorter stitch length. Try moving the hoop around in swirls, back and forth, and up and down – the stitching should be free.

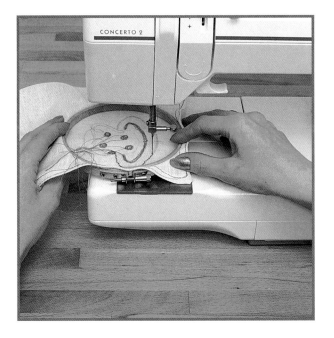

STEP FOUR

Build up your design, changing colours of thread as you need to. Swivel, rotate and slither your hoop around for the best and most comfortable direction. When you have finished all the embroidery, remove the tea towel from the hoop, trim all thread ends and iron the embroidery to neaten.

⌐11⌐
BLOCK APPLIQUE
ANIMAL QUILT

*P*atches of shirt fabric machine-stitched together
form the background to this lively farmyard quilt
which depicts animals grazing within their
patchwork meadows. A cockerel surveys his hen
and chicks while another hen broods over her eggs;
grunting pigs smile across their pens as the white
sheep follow the black ram to mischief. These
enchanting animals are easy to place, and any
small child's room or fireside sofa would
welcome this warm quilt.

Appliquéing the quilt

The materials needed for the quilt are inexpensive, comprising leftover scraps of shirting and colourful fabrics. The layers of fabric and wadding are secured together with assorted buttons, giving additional colour and texture to the completed quilt.

A variety of stitches is used to suggest the texture in each animal's coat: swirls of running stitches for the woolly sheep, cross stitch over the cats' backs with long stitches for their whiskers, and feathered blanket stitch to outline the wings of the cockerel and hens. The pigs have curved chain-stitch tails, giving them a cheeky air. The cats have three additional stitches for a detail of mouth and nose; their long exaggerated whiskers contribute to their charm. The ram and sheep are given droopy ears for a peaky look, and the ram has the addition of contrasting horns. The broody hen sits on her large eggs in a straw nest stitched with long criss-cross stitches. Each animal is securely attached to the quilt with small hemming stitches and a friendly French knot eye. Finally, all the different and varied elements of the farmyard scene are united by clusters of three or five long free stitches representing tufts of grass.

MATERIALS

Block patchwork quilt

❧

Coloured wool felt

❧

Stranded embroidery thread in varying colours

STEP ONE

Make a patchwork quilt using large rectangular blocks of different coloured fabric for the patches (refer to pages 10–20 for basic patchwork and quilting techniques). Trace the animal templates from pages 84–5, enlarge them, and then cut them out. If you are using a fabric that frays, either back it with transfer adhesive (see page 21), or allow 6mm (¼in) around the edge to turn under. Place the animal templates on the chosen colours of felt, pin to secure, then cut them out.

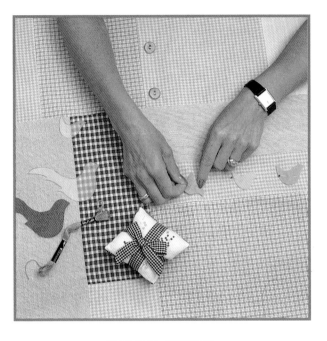

STEP TWO

Pin out all the animal designs on the patchwork quilt. Position the three chicks in a row along a narrow strip which suits their size.

STEP THREE

Cut out little legs for the chicks in contrasting bright colours; as these fabrics are liable to fray the legs were cut larger and the raw edges pinned underneath. Position the little legs so that they appear to be running, and overlap them occasionally for more movement.

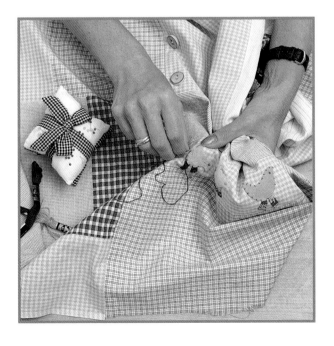

STEP FOUR

Using three strands of stranded cotton, stitch the chicks in place with small catch stitches. Choose a contrasting coloured thread for each chick. Hem around the body and down each leg.

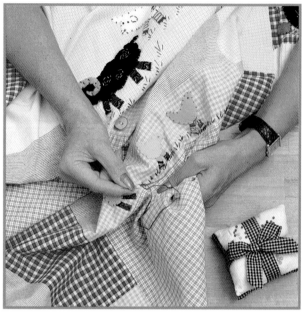

STEP FIVE

Complete each chick by stitching a French knot for the eye. To do this, bring your needle and thread out slightly to the right of where you want the knot to be. Wind the thread once around the needle and insert the needle to the left of the point where you brought it out. Do not pull the needle out too hard or the knot will disappear through the fabric.

STEP SIX

Stitch clusters of grass in tufts of three or five long free stitches around the feet of the chicks. Vary the height and length of the stitches to add a more natural feel to the grass. Stitch the rest of the animal motifs on to the quilt in a similar way to create amusing farmyard scenes.

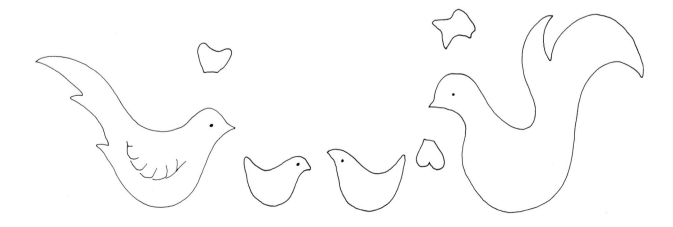

This colourful and friendly farmyard quilt depicts pigs, chickens, sheep, and cats on a patchwork base of cotton shirting.

~ 12 ~
BRIGHT APPLIQUED TOWELS

These appliquéd towels were greatly inspired by Matisse's beautifully colourful 'cut-outs', which he completed in his eighties. Towelling is available by the metre in fabric shops and is inexpensive so is perfect to have some fun with. You could personalize an entire set of towels, using a different colour for each member of the family so that the towel permanently on the bathroom floor can be easily identified.

Edging the towels

When buying towelling by the metre, remember that the edges have to be hemmed. As the towelling I bought was wide enough for two swimming towels, I made a scalloped border to finish the raw edge and to provide additional decoration; a wave design would also have been pretty but, if time is short, straight contrasting bias binding edges are very smart.

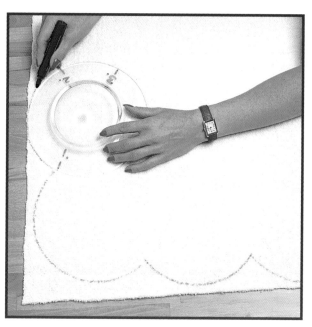

STEP ONE

Find a curve you like, such as the curved edge of a teacup or a dinner plate. Using a felt-tip pen, make a mark on the edge of the plate and label it 1; make another mark directly opposite this, and label it 3. Add another mark two-thirds of the way between the first two marks and label this 2. Lay the plate on the towelling close to the edge and draw around the edge of the plate with the felt-tip pen to create the scalloped edge. To make the corner scallop, draw a curve between marks 1 and 3.

STEP TWO

Continue marking the scallops along the edge of the towelling with the felt-tip pen, drawing around the plate between marks 1 and 2 for a gentle curve. Mark the scallop edging all the way around the towelling.

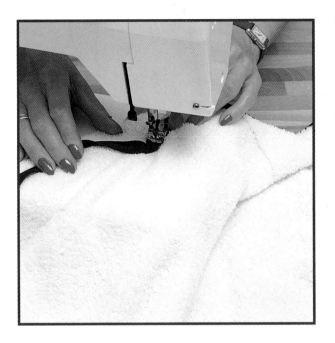

STEP THREE

Machine-stitch one edge of the bias binding along the scalloped edge of the towel, working slowly to attach the binding securely. You may want to pin the binding before stitching. The binding should cover the blue felt-tip marks as you proceed.

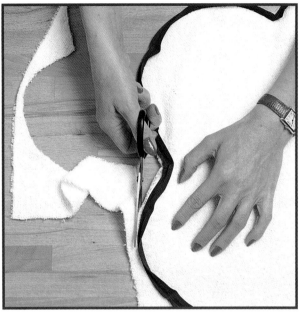

STEP FOUR

When you have stitched on the binding and all the felt-pen curves are covered, carefully cut away the excess towelling to enable you to wrap the bias binding over the edge and cover the reverse side comfortably.

STEP FIVE

Wrap the binding over the cut edge. Then either machine-stitch the bias binding down on the reverse side, or hem it in position by hand.

Attaching the seaweed motifs

Appliqué is fun and easy to do, particularly using the new bonding fabric to facilitate your work. Now there are no more fraying ends, you simply stick one fabric on to another and enjoy topstitching for additional decorative effect.

I chose a seaweed appliqué motif with which to decorate this towel because it is such a lovely shape, it can be as colourful as you like and it also has a suggestion of movement about it. You can vary the design tremendously, simply by placing the motif in different positions. Whether you choose to appliqué one motif or three, you will create instant impact. Of course, you do not have to use this seaweed template – you could design your own appliqué motif.

Whatever subject you choose as your appliqué motif, think of the possibility of movement within the design: flowers or buds opening up along a branch, fishes swimming in a shoal or twisting to follow one another up the side of a towel are a couple of examples you could use, but the possibilities for design are endless.

MATERIALS

Polyester felt in
four colours

ᘓᘔ

Towel

ᘓᘔ

Basting thread

ᘓᘔ

Matching sewing thread

STEP ONE

Either photocopy or trace the seaweed template above. If you photocopy the template, consider enlarging or reducing it to suit your needs. Cut out the seaweed motifs in the sizes chosen.

STEP TWO

Pin the seaweed motifs on to polyester felt. This is washable and does not shrink; if using a lighter material, refer to page 92. Cut out as many seaweed motifs as you require.

STEP THREE

Pin the seaweed polyester felt motifs over the towel in the positions you like. The orange design has been reversed to give more possibilities. As the seaweed design has 'fingers', I would recommend additionally basting the seaweed motifs into place.

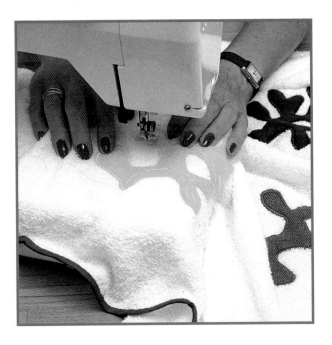

STEP FOUR

Using a sewing machine, stitch the felt seaweed motifs to the towel using matching sewing thread. Stitch around the edge of the seaweed motifs using closely-spaced zigzag stitch; you might find it helpful to use a transparent foot on your machine. To change direction when stitching, lift the machine foot leaving the needle in the fabric, and swivel the towelling around the needle. Lower the foot and begin stitching again, taking all the curves very gently and slowly. Finish off by threading loose threads through to the back of the towel.

Attaching the blue nude motif

Appliqué is a very versatile form of decoration; the blue nude motif can sunbathe, swim, dance or just sit still. Simply by repositioning the limbs you can make her move. In the same way that Matisse had experimented in his original work with 'cut-outs' and drawing pins, I decided to do the same, attaching my blue nude limbs to the towel with pins, thus giving me greater scope to play with all her many movements.

MATERIALS

Transfer adhesive

Cotton fabric or
old shirt front

Towel

Matching sewing thread

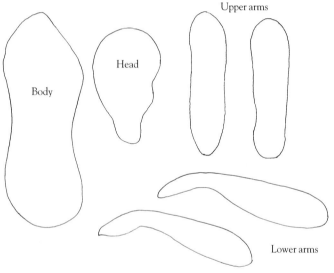

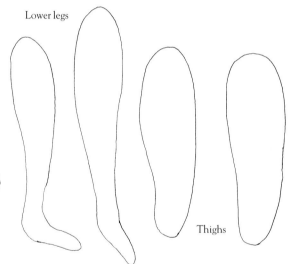

STEP ONE

Trace the blue nude template (see above) on to transfer adhesive (see page 21). Then iron the transfer adhesive on to the appliqué fabric. Cut out the appliqué motifs, leaving the paper backing in place to label the separate elements of the appliqué. One advantage of using transfer adhesive is that by peeling off the paper backing you can then place the stiffened surface of the appliqué on to the towelling and re-iron it into place. Do not do this with the blue nude, however, as some of the limbs overlap others.

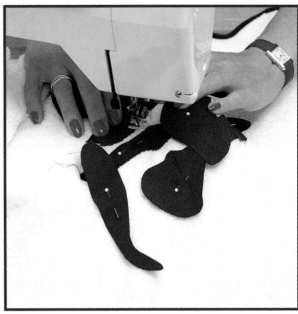

STEP TWO

Arrange the blue nude design on the towelling. Pin in place. Take care to tuck the head beneath the body to conceal the neck end, and place the far leg and arm underneath the nearer limbs. This extra attention will show in the detail of the finished work.

STEP THREE

Using matching blue thread, stitch the appliqué motifs to the towelling with closely-spaced machine zigzag stitch. You might find it helpful to use a transparent foot on your machine. If you wish to have a stitched outline on the reverse of the towelling, use a contrasting thread in the bobbin to the colour of the towelling. When stitching around tight corners, lift the presser foot while keeping the needle in the towelling and swivel the work a little on the needle. Then replace the foot and continue stitching.

STEP FOUR

Sew in all the loose thread ends to neaten the finished look. Iron the appliqué gently; the heat from the iron will cause the transfer adhesive on the back of the appliqué motifs to fuse to the towel, securing it in place.

ACKNOWLEDGEMENTS

A special thanks to Katherine and Oshi Turner for allowing three-month-old Rufus Alexander Octavian to be photographed on the baby's puff patchwork quilt. He was a delight!

For fabrics & related materials:

DMC Creative World
62 Pullman Road, Wigston,
Leicester LE18 2DY
Tel: 0116 2811040
Fax: 0116 2813592

More than 428 colours to choose from in perlé, stranded and sewing cottons. There are also wonderful Zweigart linens, counted weaves and textured fabrics; all products are fully washable. There is a comprehensive catalogue and exceptional colour sample charts availabe from DMC stockists.

Singer Sewing Machines UK Limited
Haslemere Heathrow Estate,
The Park Way,
Hounslow,
Middlesex TW4 6NQ
Tel: 0181-261 3230
Fax: 0181-261 3240

All the projects within the book were made using the Singer Concerto sewing machine, which is at the middle range of the Singer models, and is a very versatile machine.

Souleiado Provencal Fabrics
78 Rue de Seine, Paris 75006, France
Tel: 00331 43546225

My utmost thanks to Souleiado for their exceptional fabrics which are perfect for patchwork, quilting and appliqué and are used in abundance throughout this book. There are many Souleiado shops in France and capital cities around the world, featuring exquisite collections of Provençal fabrics, both traditional and contemporary designs, in all weights of material. The Souleiado shops are a feast of fabrics not to be missed.

Thomas Pink Shirts Ltd
1 Havelock Terrace, London SW8 4AP
Tel: 0171-498 2202
Fax: 0171-498 3325

My thanks to Thomas Pink Shirts for contributing to many of the projects throughout this book. The selection of colours, stripes and checks are a feast for the eyes; men look rather good in them too!

Vilene Retail
Freudenburg Nonwovens LP, PO Box 3,
Greetland, Halifax HX4 8NJ
Tel: 01422 313131
Fax: 01422 313136

Vilene has a wide selection of materials for patchwork, quilting and appliqué, plus many other new and excellent ideas for other sewing projects.

For miscellaneous props:

The Hill Toy Company
71 Abingdon Road,
London W8 6AW
Tel: 0171-937 8797
Fax: 01765 689111
Free mail order catalogue: 01765 689955

For an original selection of imaginative traditional toys, I strongly recommend a visit.

Marlow Ropes Ltd
Hailsham, East Sussex BN27 3JS
Tel: 01323 847234
Fax: 01323 440093

Vibrant, hard-wearing ropes of many dimensions that are soft to use. Excellent colour selection for easy identification and multiple usage. Available from any good chandler.

Wrentham Basketware
4-6 London Road, Wrentham,
Suffolk NR34 7HE
Tel: 01502 675628
Fax: 01493 330084

Mr Phipot made the beautiful Moses basket (see page 33) to my specifications, informing me of all the details and choices. He produces a wide selection of basketware and makes to commission.

For help with location photography:

Lymington Marina Ltd
The Shipyard, Bath Road, Lymington,
Hampshire SO41 3YL
Tel: 01590 673312
Fax: 01590 676353

I should like to thank the staff of the marina for their help during photography, and for their advice and information regarding my small boat.

TEMPLATES

The following templates can be used to create the projects in this book. They are shown actual size unless otherwise stated. To use one of these templates, carefully tear it out of the book, enlarge it if necessary, and then, referring to the particular project, photocopy the template as many times as you require, or trace over the template to make paper or postcard templates to pin on to your fabric. Remember to mark each patchwork template accurately with the colour tone and the directional arrows of the nap or pattern of the fabric. This will ensure that you pin the template correctly on the fabric. Other templates appear throughout the book within some of the projects. To use these, simply trace them and enlarge as necessary.

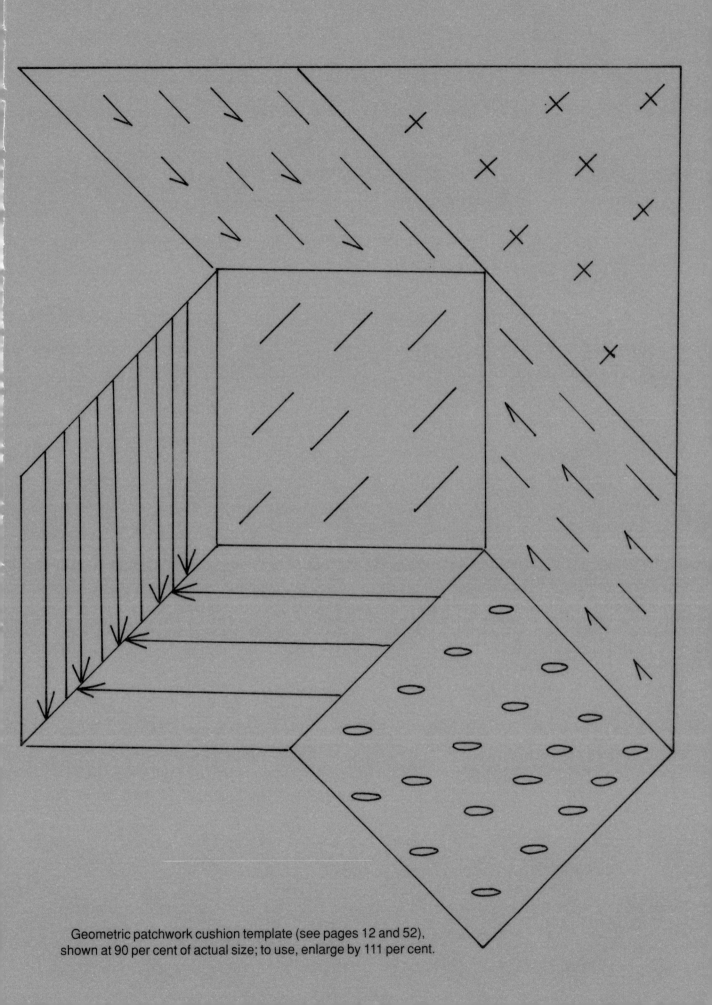

Geometric patchwork cushion template (see pages 12 and 52),
shown at 90 per cent of actual size; to use, enlarge by 111 per cent.

Geometric patchwork cushion template (see pages 12 and 52),
shown at 90 per cent of actual size; to use, enlarge by 111 per cent.

Geometric patchwork cushion template (see page 52), shown
at 90 per cent of actual size; to use, enlarge by 111 per cent.

Geometric patchwork cushion template (see page 52), shown
at 90 per cent of actual size; to use, enlarge by 111 per cent.

Geometric patchwork cushion template (see page 52), shown
at 90 per cent of actual size; to use, enlarge by 111 per cent.

Geometric patchwork cushion template (see page 52), shown
at 90 per cent of actual size; to use, enlarge by 111 per cent.

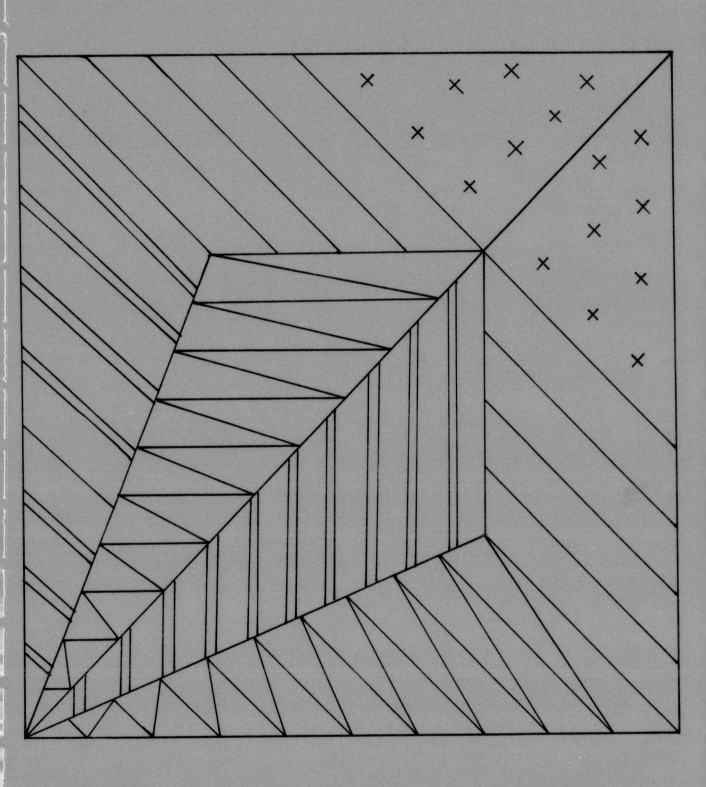

Geometric patchwork cushion template (see page 52), shown
at 90 per cent of actual size; to use, enlarge by 111 per cent.

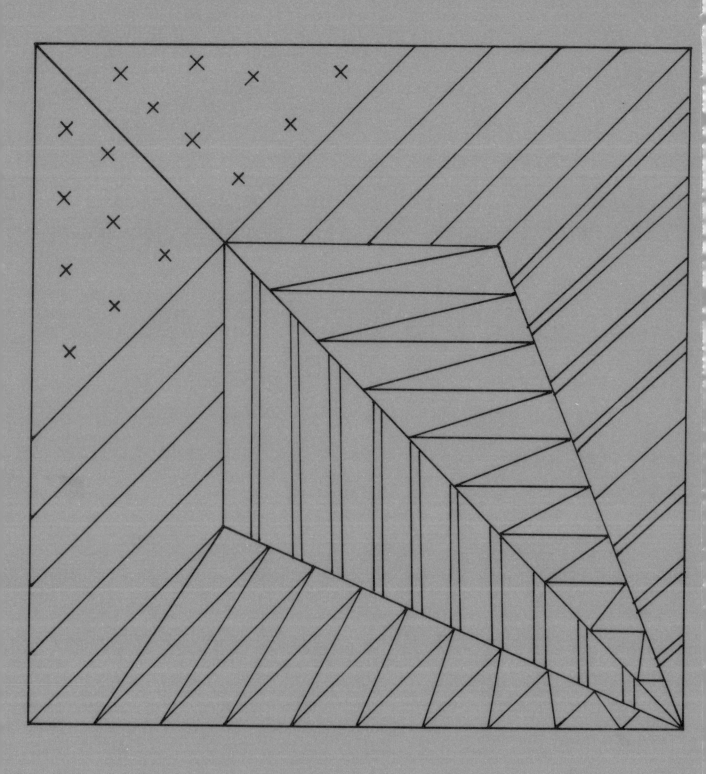

Geometric patchwork cushion template (see page 52), shown
at 90 per cent of actual size; to use, enlarge by 111 per cent.

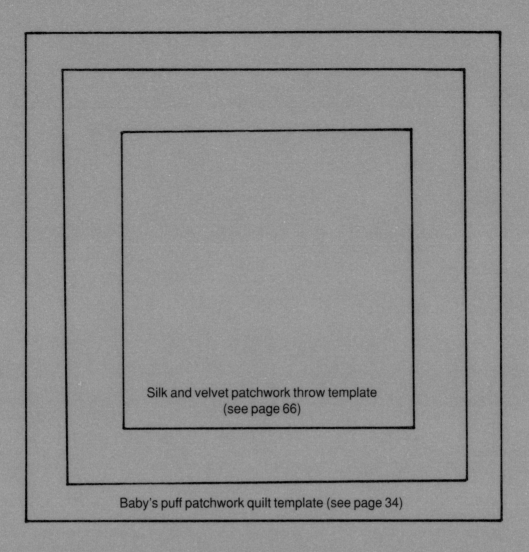

Silk and velvet patchwork throw template
(see page 66)

Baby's puff patchwork quilt template (see page 34)

Tumbling block template (see page 56)

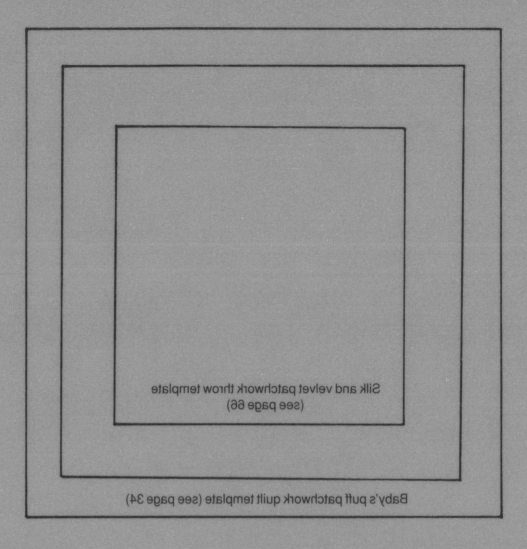

Silk and velvet patchwork throw template
(see page 66)

Baby's puff patchwork quilt template (see page 34)

Tumbling block template (see page 56)

Fruit and flowers template for hand-quilted cushion (see page 42),
shown at 90 per cent of actual size; to use, enlarge by 111 per cent.

Fruit and flowers template for hand-quilted cushion (see page 42), shown at 90 per cent of actual size; to use, enlarge by 111 per cent.

Silk patchwork cushion template (see page 60), shown at 90 per cent
of actual size; to use, enlarge by 111 per cent.

Silk patchwork cushion template (see page 60), shown at 90 per cent of actual size; to use, enlarge by 111 per cent.

Silk patchwork cushion template (see page 62)

Silk patchwork cushion template (see page 62)